INSPIRATION FOR

Girls

© 2008 by Barbour Publishing, Inc.

ISBN 978-1-60260-200-7

Some material previously published in *365 Moments of Laughter for Girlfriends*, *365 Favorite Quotes for Friends*, *365 Days of Hope*, *365 Treasured Moments for Mothers and Daughters*, *365 Secrets of Beauty*, and *365 Inspirational Quotes*. All published by Barbour Publishing, Inc.

Unless otherwise indicated, scripture quotations are taken from the Holy Bible, New Life Version, Copyright 1969, 1976, 1978, 1983, 1986, Christian Literature International, P.O. Box 777, Canby, OR 97013. Used by permission.

Scripture quotations marked NLT are taken from the *Holy Bible*, New Living Translation, copyright © 1996. Used by permission of Tyndale House Publishers, Inc. Wheaton, Illinois 60189, U.S.A. All rights reserved.

Scripture quotations marked MSG are from **THE MESSAGE.** Copyright © by Eugene H. Peterson 1993, 1994, 1995, 1996, 2000, 2001, 2002. Used by permission of NavPress Publishing Group.

Cover phtograph: James Schnepf/The Image Bank/Getty Images

Published by Barbour Publishing, Inc., P.O. Box 719, Uhrichsville, Ohio 44683, www.barbourbooks.com

Our mission is to publish and distribute inspirational products offering exceptional value and biblical encouragement to the masses.

Printed in China.

INSPIRATION FOR

Girls

BARBOUR

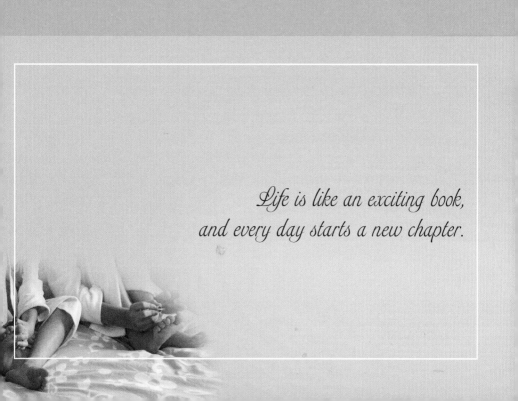

*Life is like an exciting book,
and every day starts a new chapter.*

"*For* I know the plans I have for you,"
says the Lord, "plans for well-being and not for trouble,
to give you a future and a hope."

JEREMIAH 29:11

The moment we asked Jesus to forgive us,
we became blemish-free on the inside.

*The stars exist that we might know
how high our dreams can soar.*

*K*ind words can be short and easy to speak,
but their echoes are truly endless.

MOTHER TERESA

God's promises are like the stars;
  the darker the night the brighter they shine.

DAVID NICHOLAS

GOD is all mercy and grace—
not quick to anger, is rich in love.

PSALM 145:8 MSG

$\mathcal{N}$o one is useless in this world who lightens the burdens of another.

CHARLES DICKENS

You are God's created beauty and the focus of His affection and delight.

JANET L. WEAVER

$\mathcal{W}$hy did God make mothers? To teach us how to love Him. To teach us how to love.

LARISSA CARRICK

*There is something in every season,
in every day, to celebrate with thanksgiving.*

GLORIA GAITHER

Having someone who understands you is home.
Having someone who loves you is belonging.
Having both is a blessing.

God will never, never, never let us down
if we have faith and put our trust in Him.
He will always look after us.

MOTHER TERESA

You can trust God right now to supply all your needs for today. And if your needs are bigger tomorrow, His supply will be bigger also.

God has designed you wonderfully well. He thinks about you every minute of every day. He has a special purpose just for you, a niche that only you can fill.

LORI SHANKLE

*I can do all things because
Christ gives me the strength.*

PHILIPPIANS 4:13

$\mathcal{O}$ne thing I'd give my friend, if I could give you one thing, I would wish for you the ability to see yourself as others see you. Then you would realize what a truly special person you are.

B. A. BILLINGSLY

God has always used ordinary people
to carry out His extraordinary mission.

Where there is great love, there are miracles.

WILLA CATHER

You cannot do a kindness too soon because
you never know how soon it will be too late.

RALPH WALDO EMERSON

Joy is not in things, it is in us.

RICHARD WAGNER

If one life shines,
the life next to it will catch the light.

ANONYMOUS

God thinks you're marvelous!
He created you exactly how you are.

One kind word can warm three winter months.

JAPANESE PROVERB

$\mathcal{M}$ay God send His love like sunshine
in His warm and gentle way to fill each corner
of your heart each moment of today.

$\mathcal{I}$ will give thanks to the Lord with all my heart.
I will tell of all the great things You have done.

PSALM 9:1

To fall down you manage alone,
but it takes loving hands to get up.

YIDDISH PROVERB

If you can eat today, enjoy the sunlight today,
mix good cheer with friends today,
enjoy it, and bless God for it.

HENRY WARD BEECHER

Give to the world the best you know,
and the best will come back to you.

HENRY WADSWORTH LONGFELLOW

Laughter is the sun that drives winter from the face.

VICTOR HUGO

You are a child of the Most High King.
God has crowned you with His favor.

*H*appiness is something to do,
something to love, something to hope for.

CHINESE PROVERB

If you can walk, you can dance.
If you can talk, you can sing.

ZIMBABWE PROVERB

Every day holds the possibility of a miracle.

$\mathcal{A}$ little of what you fancy does you good.

MARIE LLOYD

Be happy in the Lord.
And He will give you the desires of your heart.

PSALM 37:4

Sometimes mothers are quiet,
standing in the background, but you know
they're always there for you.

I believe in the sun when it is not shining.

I believe in love even when I do not feel it.

I believe in God even when He is silent.

$\mathcal{A}$ friend is someone who knows the song in your heart and can sing it back to you when you have forgotten the words.

UNKNOWN

Little deeds of kindness, little words of love,
help to make earth happy like the heaven above.

JULIA A. FLETCHER CARNEY

I want to help you to grow as beautiful as
God meant you to be when He thought of you first.

GEORGE MACDONALD

Salt is like good humor,
and nearly everything is better [with] a pinch of it.

LOUISA MAY ALCOTT

I will not be afraid of anything,
because (God is) with me.

PSALM 23:4

Choose happiness today!
It's a beautiful life!

$\mathcal{N}$o act of kindness,
no matter how small, is ever wasted.

AESOP

Friends. . .they cherish each other's hopes.
They are kind to each other's dreams.

HENRY DAVID THOREAU

What you are becoming is more important
than what you are accomplishing.

$\mathcal{T}$here is nothing like a dream
to create the future.

VICTOR HUGO

Don't fear tomorrow;
God is already there.

The most beautiful things cannot be seen
or even touched. They must be felt with the heart.

HELEN KELLER

*Lovely flowers are the smiles
of God's goodness.*

WILLIAM WILBERFORCE

$\mathcal{P}$romise only what you can give.
Then give more than you promise.

UNKNOWN

*Come close to God and He
will come close to you.*

JAMES 4:8

*I*n nature, nothing is perfect
and everything is perfect. Trees can be contorted,
bent in weird ways, and they're still beautiful.

ALICE WALKER

Home is where they love you.

UNKNOWN

$\mathcal{P}$ractice hope. As hopefulness becomes a habit,
you can achieve a permanently happy spirit.

NORMAN VINCENT PEALE

A real friend is one who walks in when the rest of the world walks out.

WALTER WINCHELL

Be great in little things.

FRANCIS XAVIER

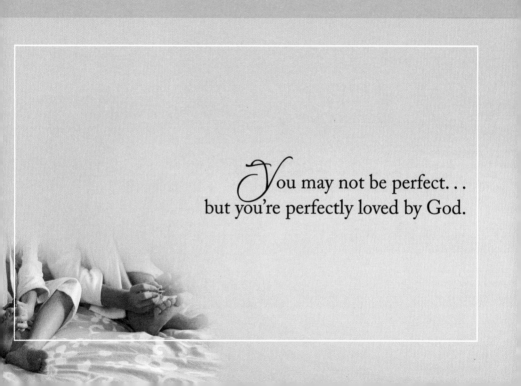

*Y*ou may not be perfect...
but you're perfectly loved by God.

*L*aughter is the closest thing
to the grace of God.

KARL BARTH

Silent gratitude isn't much use to anyone.

G. B. STERN

*E*ach little flower that opens,
each little bird that sings,
God made their glowing colors,
He made their tiny wings.

CECIL FRANCES ALEXANDER

$\mathcal{A}$nyone who belongs to Christ has
become a new person. The old life
is gone; a new life has begun!

2 CORINTHIANS 5:17 NLT

Love is the beauty of the soul.

SAINT AUGUSTINE

*T*reasure your relationships,
not your possessions.

ANTHONY J. D'ANGELO

The heart sees better than the eye.

JEWISH PROVERB

Some people come into our lives and quickly go.
Some stay for a while and leave footprints on our hearts.
And we are never, ever the same.

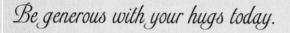

Be generous with your hugs today.

To accomplish great things,
we must dream as well as act.

ANATOLE FRANCE

Little girls with dreams become women with vision.

UNKNOWN

$\mathcal{W}$e can totally be ourselves with God.
He knows us inside and out—after all, He made us!

A gentle word, a kind look, a good-natured smile can work wonders and accomplish miracles.

WILLIAM HAZLITT

$\mathcal{F}$or the Lord is happy with His people.
He saves those who have no pride
and makes them beautiful.

PSALM 149:4

*Write it on your heart that every day
is the best day of the year.*

RALPH WALDO EMERSON

Even if you hate your freckles or wish you were taller, God thinks you're perfect. He adores you, and He wants you to find out just how much.

*The creation of a thousand forests
is in one acorn.*

RALPH WALDO EMERSON

Courage is the capacity to go ahead in spite of the fear.

SCOTT PECK

*F*aith makes all things possible.
Hope makes all things bright.
Love makes all things easy.

If we did all the things we are capable of doing,
we would literally astound ourselves.

THOMAS EDISON

Hold a true friend with both your hands.

NIGERIAN PROVERB

Every person's life is a fairy tale
written by God's fingers.

HANS CHRISTIAN ANDERSEN

A smile is an inexpensive way to improve your looks.

God has chosen you.
You are holy and loved by Him.

COLOSSIANS 3:12

$\mathcal{Y}$ou see things; and you say, "Why?" But I dream things that never were; and I say, "Why not?"

GEORGE BERNARD SHAW

It's easier to believe in yourself when you have a friend beside you saying, "I believe in you, too."

BONNIE JENSEN

$\mathcal{L}$ife dances with those already on the dance floor.

UNKNOWN

God adores you, and He always has.

*I*t isn't what you have in your pocket that makes you thankful, but what you have in your heart.

UNKNOWN

Love isn't how you feel. It's what you do.

MADELEINE L'ENGLE

God loves each one of us as if there were only one of us.

ST. AUGUSTINE

$\mathcal{P}$eople who judge don't matter.
People who matter don't judge.

UNKNOWN

Happiness is what happens to us when we try to make someone else happy.

UNKNOWN

If we learn how to give ourselves,
to forgive others, and to live with thanksgiving,
we need not seek happiness. It will seek us.

There can be no happiness equal to the joy of finding a heart that understands.

VICTOR ROBINSALL

$\mathcal{F}$riends touch our lives in ways no one else can. . . .
They leave lasting imprints on our hearts.

KELLY WILLIAMS

*Y*our beauty should come from the inside.
It should come from the heart. This is the kind
that lasts. Your beauty should be a gentle and
quiet spirit. In God's sight this is of great worth
and no amount of money can buy it.

1 PETER 3:4

*It isn't the great big pleasures that count the most;
it's making a great deal out of the little ones.*

JEAN WEBSTER

*A*nyone can give up; it's the easiest thing in the world to do. But to hold it together when everyone else would understand if you fell apart, that's true strength.

*I*t was only a sunny smile, and little it cost in the giving. But like morning light, it scattered the night, and made the day worth living.

UNKNOWN

Sometimes the only sense you can make
out of life is a sense of humor.

UNKNOWN

*Those who are filled with love
are filled with God Himself.*

SAINT AUGUSTINE

Friendship is a cozy shelter
from life's rainy days.

UNKNOWN

$\mathcal{L}$et us be grateful to people who make us happy; they are the charming gardeners who make our souls blossom.

MARCEL PROUST

When I count my blessings,
I always count my friends twice.

UNKNOWN

You won't realize the distance you've walked until you take a look around and realize how far you've been.

My soul will be happy in the Lord.
It will be full of joy because He saves.

PSALM 35:9

*I*f you can imagine it, you can achieve it.
If you can dream it, you can become it.

WILLIAM ARTHUR WARD

Modesty is the noblest of all ornaments.

ELEAZER ROKEACH

$\mathcal{F}$riends are angels with hidden wings.

SUSAN DUKE

If you see a friend without a smile,
give her one of yours.

The moments of happiness we enjoy take us by surprise.
It is not that we seize them, but that they seize us.

ASHLEY MONTAGU

Life isn't about the breaths we take,
but the moments that take our breath away.

UNKNOWN

$\mathcal{M}$ay the sun always shine on your windowpane;
   may a rainbow be certain to follow each rain;
   may the hand of a friend always be near you;
may God fill your heart with gladness to cheer you.

IRISH BLESSING

Friendship is the sort of love one can imagine between angels.

C. S. LEWIS

$\mathcal{T}$hose who bring sunshine to the lives of others
cannot keep it from themselves.

J. M. BARRIE

$\mathcal{G}$od is keeping careful watch over us
and the future. The Day is coming when you'll
have it all—life healed and whole.

1 PETER 1:5 MSG

The strongest people aren't always the people who win,
but the people who don't give up when they lose.

ASHLEY HODGESON

$\mathcal{W}$alking with a friend in the dark
is better than walking alone in the light.

HELEN KELLER

The heart that loves is always young.

GREEK PROVERB

*To love and be loved is
to feel the sun from both sides.*

DAVID VISCOTT

You don't have to worry about impressing God. He already thinks you're great—even when you first get up in the morning. Now that's real love!

I like the dreams of the future better than the history of the past.

THOMAS JEFFERSON

*J*ust thinking about a friend makes you want to do a happy dance, because a friend is someone who loves you in spite of your faults.

CHARLES M. SHULZ

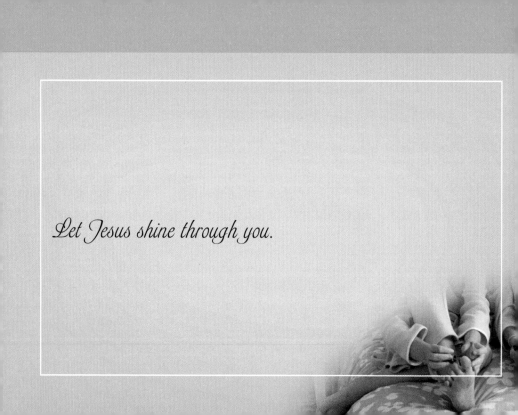

Let Jesus shine through you.

*U*se what talents you possess:
the woods would be very silent if no birds
sang there except those that sang best.

HENRY VAN DYKE

I will put my hope in God!

PSALM 42:11 NLT

$\mathcal{N}$o one can go back and make a brand-new start,
but anyone can start from now and
make a brand-new ending.

*B*ig doesn't necessarily mean better.
Sunflowers aren't better than violets.

EDNA FERBER

Joy lights the world one grin at a time!

$\mathcal{T}$he finger of God touches your life
when you make a friend.

MARY DAWSON HUGHES

Innocence is like polished armor;
it adorns and defends.

BISHOP ROBERT SOUTH

$\mathcal{E}$mbrace the wonder and excitement each day brings.
For tomorrow affords us new opportunities...
Time to experience... Time to create...
Time to reflect... Time to dream.

You are a beautiful princess—
a member of God's royal family.

Happiness is a habit; cultivate it.

ELBERT HUBBARD

*W*hen the world says, "Give up," God whispers, "Try it one more time."

*L*augh with your happy friends when they're happy;
share tears when they're down.

ROMANS 12:15 MSG

Shoot for the moon. Even if you miss,
you'll land among the stars.

LES BROWN

Take time to play. It is the secret of perpetual youth.
Take time to laugh. It is the music of the soul.

OLD ENGLISH PROVERB

Love comforteth like sunshine after rain.

WILLIAM SHAKESPEARE

Cheerfulness is the atmosphere
in which all things thrive.

JOHANN PAUL RICHTER

One can bear grief,
but it takes two to be glad.

ELBERT HUBBARD

Laugh often.
Dream big.
Reach for the stars!

$\mathcal{A}$ngels fly because they take themselves lightly.

UNKNOWN

*When a great adventure is offered,
don't refuse it.*

AMELIA EARHART

$\mathcal{W}$e should be thankful for those people
who rekindle the inner spirit.

ALBERT SCHWEITZER

"*N*o eye has ever seen or no ear has ever heard or no mind has ever thought of the wonderful things God has made ready for those who love Him."

1 CORINTHIANS 2:9

*B*e the living expression of God's kindness: kindness in your face, kindness in your eyes, kindness in your smile.

MOTHER TERESA

A faithful friend is an image of God.

FRENCH PROVERB

$\mathcal{T}$he reason birds can fly and we can't
is simply that they have perfect faith,
for to have faith is to have wings.

J. M. BARRIE

Everyone was meant to share God's all-abiding love and care; He saw that we would need to know a way to let these feelings show. . .so God made hugs.

JILL WOLF

Treat your friends as you do your pictures and place them in their best light.

SIR WINSTON CHURCHILL

'Tis a lesson you should heed: Try, try, try again.
If at first you don't succeed, Try, try, try again.

W. E. HICKSON

$\mathcal{D}$on't cry because it's over.
Smile because it happened.

DR. SEUSS

Some seek happiness.
Others create it.

Unshared joy is an unlighted candle.

SPANISH PROVERB

*L*et your light shine in front of men.
Then they will see the good things you do
and will honor your Father Who is in heaven.

MATTHEW 5:16

A friend is someone who understands your past, believes in your future, and accepts you just the way you are.

Everyone is beautiful when sharing laughter.

UNKNOWN

$\mathcal{F}$riendship is the only cement that
will ever hold the world together.

WOODROW WILSON

*E*very experience God gives us, every person
He puts into our lives, is the perfect
preparation for the future that only He can see.

CORRIE TEN BOOM

$\mathcal{P}$eople are like stained-glass windows:
They sparkle and shine when the sun is out,
but when the darkness sets in, their true beauty
is revealed only if there is a light within.

ELISABETH KÜBLER-ROSS

Best friends are like diamonds,
precious but rare.

UNKNOWN

$\mathcal{G}$od has given us two hands—
one to receive with and the other to give with.

BILLY GRAHAM

Any day is sunny that is brightened by a smile.

UNKNOWN

$\mathcal{A}$ real friend is not so much someone you feel free to be serious with as someone you feel free to be silly with.

SYDNEY J. HARRIS

*H*ave your roots planted deep in Christ.
Grow in Him. Get your strength from Him.
Let Him make you strong in the faith
as you have been taught.

COLOSSIANS 2:7

The first duty of love is to listen.

PAUL TILLICH

Laughter is the spark of the soul.

UNKNOWN

*H*appiness is like jam. You can't spread even a little without getting some on yourself.

UNKNOWN

*T*here are certain things in life that can't be [overdone]—smiling, giving, caring, loving, being thankful, and being a good friend.

BONNIE JENSEN

Imagination is everything.
It is the preview of life's coming attractions.

ALBERT EINSTEIN

The wings of prayer can carry high and far.

ANONYMOUS

You cannot always have happiness,
but you can always give happiness.

UNKNOWN

*Y*our love will make the God in you
so attractive, people will be curious about you.
They'll want to know what makes you different—
why you stand out in a crowd. And you can
share the answer—Jesus!

A smile gently hugs the heart of the one who receives it.

UNKNOWN

$\mathcal{H}$e who asks a question is a fool for five minutes;
he who does not ask a question remains a fool forever.

CHINESE PROVERB

The heart that loves is always young.

GREEK PROVERB

God is with us, and His power is around us.

CHARLES H. SPURGEON

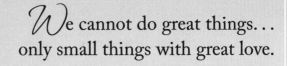

$\mathcal{W}$e cannot do great things. . .
only small things with great love.

MOTHER TERESA

God's hand is always there; once you grab it,
He'll never let go.

*T*he world is good-natured to people
who are good-natured.

WILLIAM MAKEPEACE THACKERAY

The beauty of a woman is not in the clothes
she wears, the figure that she carries, or the way
she combs her hair. The beauty of a woman must
be seen from in her eyes, because that is the doorway
to her heart, the place where love resides.

AUDREY HEPBURN

The greatest sweetener of human life is friendship.

JOSEPH ADDISON

You are not called to be a canary
in a cage. You are called to be an eagle,
and to fly sun to sun, over continents.

HENRY WARD BEECHER

$\mathcal{T}$o have a good friend is one of the highest delights of life; to be a good friend is one of the noblest undertakings.

UNKNOWN

*W*e must remember what the Lord Jesus said, "We are more happy when we give than when we receive."

ACTS 20:35

While our hearts are pure, our lives are happy and our peace is sure.

WILLIAM WINTER